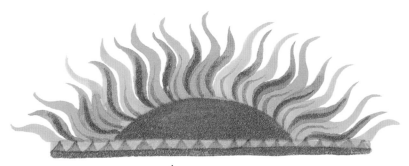

Earth,
Fire,
Water,
Air

For our children,

Sarah–Rhiannon, Rebecca, Jessica, Clara, Ellen, and Joseph,

and for all the others who will inherit the earth

Text copyright © 1995 by Mary Hoffman
Illustrations copyright © 1995 by Jane Ray

First published in the United States 1995 by Dutton Children's Books,
a division of Penguin Books USA Inc.
375 Hudson Street, New York, New York 10014

Originally published in Great Britain 1995 by Orion Children's Books, London

"Buffalo Dusk" from *Smoke and Steel* by Carl Sandburg,
copyright © 1920 by Harcourt Brace & Company and renewed 1948
by Carl Sandburg, reprinted by permission of the publisher.

"Little Fish" by D. H. Lawrence, from *The Complete Poems of D. H. Lawrence*,
edited by V. de Sola Pinto & F. W. Roberts. Copyright © 1964, 1971 by Angelo Ravagli
and C. M. Weekley, Executors of the Estate of Frieda Lawrence Ravagli. Used by permission
of Viking Penguin, a division of Penguin Books USA Inc.

Typography by Semadar Megged
Printed and bound in Italy
First American Edition
ISBN 0-525-45420-9
1 3 5 7 9 10 8 6 4 2

EARTH,
FIRE,
WATER,
AIR

by MARY HOFFMAN ◆ illustrated by JANE RAY

DUTTON CHILDREN'S BOOKS • NEW YORK

CONTENTS

INTRODUCTION

The song of the earth has been sung since the beginning of time, but we can no longer hear it. Through exploring the magic of earth, fire, water, and air, the words of that song may return to us, and perhaps we can learn the tune again. Most of us, living in our centrally heated homes with their modern kitchens and bathrooms, are out of touch with the four elements and never see their links with nature. Yet earth, fire, water, and air still hold strong magic and are the key to a rich world of stories, legends, pictures, and music.

People who lived thousands of years ago were in much closer touch with these four "elements" of life. That word, *elements*, was first used to describe earth, fire, water, and air 2,500 years ago, by a man named Empedocles, who lived in Greece. In his time you could not take the elements for granted. They were matters of life and death, just as they still are in many parts of the world.

Everyone needed fertile earth to grow food crops for themselves and to give grass for their animals. So they believed in a great mother goddess who gave birth to every living plant. But without water the crops and grass couldn't grow, so people performed ceremonies and spells to make the rain come. Drinking water had to be carried from springs and wells. These sources of water were so important that people believed each had its own god. Fire was a precious thing, to be kept burning in people's homes, to give not only warmth but light and heat for cooking. The ability to make fire was one of the skills that set people apart from animals. And air was the most mysterious element of all. Everyone needed it in order to live, and yet they could not see it; it was somehow connected to the sky, where all the gods lived with the winds, their servants.

Empedocles didn't think the elements were only outside of us. He believed that people, animals, and objects were all composed of a mixture of two or more elements. His ideas were accepted for hundreds of years. In the Middle Ages, in Europe, people still believed in the presence of the four elements in human beings.

Your personality, or "humour," depended on which element had the upper hand. A "fiery" person would be quick-tempered and ambitious; an "airy" one would be creative and cheerful; an "earthy" one placid and reliable; and a "watery" one thoughtful and inclined to be sad. All twelve signs of the zodiac are associated with an element, three signs to each one. Earth signs, for example, are Taurus, Virgo, and Capricorn. If you are born "under" one of these signs (determined by your date of birth) you are supposed to have "earthy" characteristics.

You don't have to believe in any of this to find it fascinating. Myths, legends, riddles, proverbs, and superstitions expressing beliefs about the four elements lie deep in the art and literature of the Western world. There are interesting and exciting beliefs about the elements in many other cultures, too. We have included stories and images from cultures that do not share in the Western tradition of four elements. Some belief systems divide the world into two, like the Chinese concept of yin and yang. Water and earth are yin, or female, while air and fire are the masculine yang forces.

There is such a rich world of ideas and images connected with the four elements that no book can include all of them. But here you can explore in words and pictures at least some of the power and mystery, the exhilaration and danger of being close to the four elements.

We human beings have so lost touch with the elements that many of us haven't noticed what our "advanced" cultures are doing to them. We have poisoned the earth, polluted the water and air with our chemicals and industries, and used fire to lay waste to acres of rain forest and grazing ground—all in the name of progress and civilization.

Let us try to recapture a sense of wonder at these four elements of life. If we feel closer to the earth, we will feel more reverence for trees and for every growing thing. If we respect fire, we will not use it so destructively. If we recognize the life-giving qualities of water, we will be ashamed to dump garbage and waste into rivers and seas. If we believe that the air is the source of all life, we will try harder to keep it clean and good to breathe.

As you discover the thrill of volcanoes and earthquakes, the mystery of drowned cities, and the beauty of legends about rainbows and Starpeople, you can join in celebrating the magic of earth, fire, water, and air. You can join in the song of the earth.

EARTH

MOTHER EARTH

Earth is the first and most important element. The Greeks and Romans named our planet after it. In the Middle Ages, it was considered the central element of the four. It is easy to see why many people thought of the earth as their first mother, the source of all life. The Greeks called her Gaia; she was Prithivi to the Hindus and Ishtar to the Babylonians. People all over the world, from North America to Japan, Scandinavia to New Zealand, believed in an earth mother-goddess and a sky father. In ancient Egypt it was the other way around: Geb was the earth god and Nut the sky goddess.

Women who wanted babies and women who were about to give birth pressed themselves close to the ground to share in her fruitfulness. Until quite recently, in one part of Italy, newborn babies were placed on the earth as soon as they had been bathed and dressed. It was a way of saying that all life comes from the earth, our mother.

All the food that people eat either grows from the soil or comes from animals, which themselves rely on the earth to provide their food. Even the birds of the air and the fishes of the sea depend on food that comes from the earth.

Gradually, though, we seem to have forgotten that the earth is the mother of us all.

15

LIFE IN THE DARK

The earth is a generous mother. Her warm embrace gives shelter to many kinds of animals. Some of the most humble are the most important, like the common earthworm. Earth passes through its body as it wriggles through the ground, breaking up the soil as it goes, making it crumbly and diggable.

Bigger animals make tunnels under the earth, forming intricate patterns, like the warrens of rabbits or the underground labyrinths of meerkats, moles, and badgers. These are the places where they sleep, give birth, and hide from predators.

16

DIGGERS AND DELVERS

But it is not just animals that burrow and tunnel into the earth. In the Ice Age, people lived in underground caves. Caves have been found in France painted with the images of bison and antelope and all the other animals that Ice Age people hunted for food. These painted caves were magical places where young boys were brought when they came of age to be hunters.

Thousands of years later, people found out that the earth mother had many treasures hidden inside her—gold, silver, diamonds, and coal—that could only be seized from her by those who would go down into the dark.   She takes many lives in return for the riches people dig out of her.

CREATURES OF THE EARTH

The earth has her own creatures, special to her, the earthbound ones who cannot fly or swim. Above all others, the bull symbolizes the strength and solidity of the earth, and carries its own magic. Even today, conjurors still use the word *abracadabra*, which comes from an ancient phrase meaning "the bull, the only bull," when they want to create a magical illusion.

Buffalo Dusk

The buffaloes are gone.
And those who saw the buffaloes are gone.
Those who saw the buffaloes by thousands and how they pawed the
    prairie sod into dust with their hoofs, their great heads down
    pawing on in a great pageant of dusk,
Those who saw the buffaloes are gone.
And the buffaloes are gone.

CARL SANDBURG

Earth's animals, the large meat eaters and the animals they feed on, the hoofed and
the horned, need a lot of room. But the open spaces are shrinking, and the animals
are disappearing, too.

19

As if the earth did not give rise to enough wonderful creatures naturally, myth and legend have given us even more miraculous beasts. The unicorn might be an elegant interpretation of the rhinoceros, or it might be a result of the belief that everything on land had its counterpart in the sea. When spiraled narwhal horns were washed up on beaches, people of the Middle Ages deduced there must be a single-horned animal on the earth, too.

The centaur was a creature of Greek myth, a man from the waist up fused with the body of a horse. It was probably the result of people seeing men riding horses for the first time.

The Sphinx was made up of parts of other animals. The Greek Sphinx has a woman's head and breasts, a lion's body, an eagle's wings, and a serpent's tail. The Egyptian Sphinx has a lion's body and a man's head.

The Chimera was an incredible mixture of lion, dragon, and she-goat. According to myth, it terrorized the people of Lycia in Asia Minor until it was killed by Bellerophon.

EARTHQUAKES

The earth is not always a gentle and loving mother; sometimes she can be terrifying and destructive. Suddenly, often without warning, the ground begins to shake and rumble and the earth splits open, swallowing anything in the way.

Some earthquakes strike in remote, uninhabited places—they can even happen under the sea. But others attack crowded cities like Los Angeles and Tokyo. It is becoming possible to predict earthquakes and to make buildings earthquake-proof. But even in earlier times, when there was no chance of avoiding or predicting earthquakes, people would always come back and build again in the same spot.

DRAGON'S TEETH

The one thing that the fruitful earth cannot produce is living creatures, though many legends say she can. One of them tells of the Greek hero Cadmus, who made men spring out of the earth. When he arrived in the land where he was to build the city of Thebes, he was thirsty. He tried to drink water from a spring, not realizing it was sacred to the war god, Ares, who had put a huge dragon to guard it. Cadmus killed the dragon so that he could drink, and Ares never forgave him.

Then the goddess Athena, who had been watching, told Cadmus to take the teeth of the dragon and plant them in the earth like seeds. When he obeyed her, a host of armed warriors immediately sprang up—too many for Cadmus to command. He threw a stone among them, and they quarreled over who had done it, killing one another until there were only five of them left. These five followed

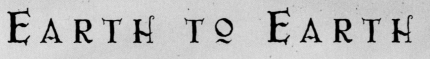

EARTH TO EARTH

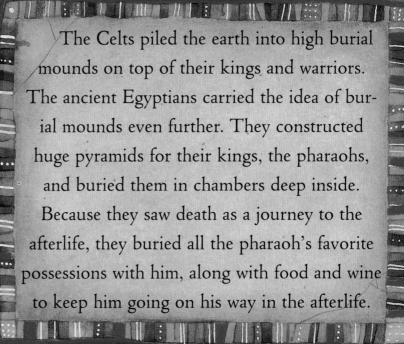

Perhaps because of a belief that the earth could give life to anything, people in many cultures have buried their dead since prehistoric times. If mother earth could bring back flowers and crops and trees after the dead period of winter, perhaps she could bring her human children back to life, too.

The Christian burial service still says "Earth to earth, ashes to ashes, dust to dust; in sure and certain hope of the Resurrection to eternal life."

The Celts piled the earth into high burial mounds on top of their kings and warriors. The ancient Egyptians carried the idea of burial mounds even further. They constructed huge pyramids for their kings, the pharaohs, and buried them in chambers deep inside. Because they saw death as a journey to the afterlife, they buried all the pharaoh's favorite possessions with him, along with food and wine to keep him going on his way in the afterlife.

25

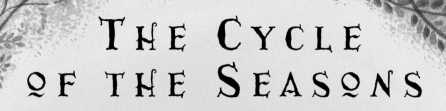

THE CYCLE
OF THE SEASONS

Life comes back out of the earth every spring. Many myths and legends around the world arose from attempts to explain this annual miracle. The Greek goddess of corn, Demeter, was the granddaughter of great mother earth herself. Demeter had a daughter, named Persephone, whose father was Zeus, the king of the gods. Persephone was stolen by Hades, the god of the underworld, to be his wife. Demeter made Zeus get her daughter back for her. But because Persephone had eaten six pomegranate seeds when she was in the underworld, she was allowed to live on earth for only six months of the year. During the other six months, she had to go back and be queen to Hades. Her mother missed her so much that the leaves fell off the trees and the earth was as bleak and miserable as Demeter felt. And that is one explanation of the seasons. Because most trees seem to die in the winter and come back to life in the spring, they have always seemed magical, symbols of everlasting life.

Trees, eternal attempts by the earth
To speak to the listening sky.

RABINDRANATH TAGORE

26

Many trees live for hundreds of years, much longer than people. Because a tree has its roots in the earth but reaches high up into the sky with its branches, it is also a symbol of striving for higher and better things. To the Celts, the oak tree was sacred; for Indians, it was the fig tree. In the lands where the Vikings came from, people believed that the whole world was supported by a great ash tree. Its name was Yggdrasil. At the bottom, coiled around its roots, lay a dragon, the Nidhogg. At the top was an eagle; in between them scurried the squirrel Ratatösk, carrying their insults back and forth. Yggdrasil's roots went down into Niflheim and up into Asgard, where the gods lived. The ash tree was believed to have been there forever and would never die.

SAVING THE EARTH

If the earth is our mother, we have treated her very badly. We have moved a long way from the native North American who refused even to dig in the earth, saying that it would mean wounding his mother. Now many parts of the world that were once full of trees have become deserts where nothing grows and nothing can live.

Large areas of rain forest in the Amazon, Madagascar, Rwanda, and other places have been burned or cut down. Often people need land for farming and cannot afford to proceed more slowly or to think about the future; they need food for their families *now*. Around the world so much is being lost—wildlife and its habitats, traditional ways of life—that it seems time is running out for many of the treasures of the earth, unless countries can work together to preserve them.

But the solutions to big problems often begin with something small. In India, the Chipko movement began when women in a village put their arms around the trees that were about to be cut down to make way for a factory. They told the woodcutters they would have to saw through them, too. The women had seen how cutting down lots of trees led to floods, which washed away roads and bridges. Now the Chipko (Hug the Tree) movement has spread all over India. It is a case of ordinary people making a real change in what is happening to the earth.

FIRE

AROUND THE FIRE

The secret of making fire is one of the skills that sets people apart from animals. We can summon fire as we wish and make it cook our food, keep us warm, even destroy for us if we want it to. Yet you might live all your life in a modern house and never see a flame.

There is something special about firelight and candlelight. They take us back to a time when fire warded off wild animals. Everyone loves a log fire, a campfire, or a bonfire, because they give us back the feeling of adventure, of being close to nature. Candles in a church symbolize the soul, the undying spirit of a human being. We make a wish when we blow out our birthday candles, perhaps to celebrate surviving for another year. Part of the magic of candles and torches comes from being able to see how vulnerable a flame is. It can be blown out by the wind or a human breath. Human life can seem just as fragile and easily snuffed out.

Fire Mountains

Fire is not always tame and comforting. There are stories of twinkling fires, called will-o'-the-wisps, that lead people to their deaths in the marshes. When fire is out of control, it can be the most terrifying of the four elements. Forest fires that rage wildly leave nothing in their path.

The most fearsome of all natural
fires comes from the heart of a volcano. The Hindus of Java believe that a
god lives inside the fire mountain, which is
what they call a volcano. They can grow three crops
of rice a year from the fertile soil on a volcano's slopes,
full of ashes from old eruptions. Even if their fire mountain
has erupted quite recently, they still climb up to the crater every year
to throw in offerings to the god, in thanks for the rich harvest. People
always want to live on and near volcanoes, because the land is good, even
though they never know when the air will be suddenly filled with fire and boiling lava.

NIGHT FIRES

There is nothing quite so magical as the contrast between a bright light and the night sky. The first night fires were the moon and stars, and there are enough stories about them to fill many books. If you look at the sky on a clear night at the right time of year, you can see some of the signs of the zodiac, such as the Crab, the Bull, and the Water Bearer. You can see Greek heroes, such as Orion, the hunter, and Perseus, who killed the Medusa; animals, such as Pegasus and the Great Bear; and women as beautiful as their names—Andromeda, Cassiopeia, and the Pleiades.

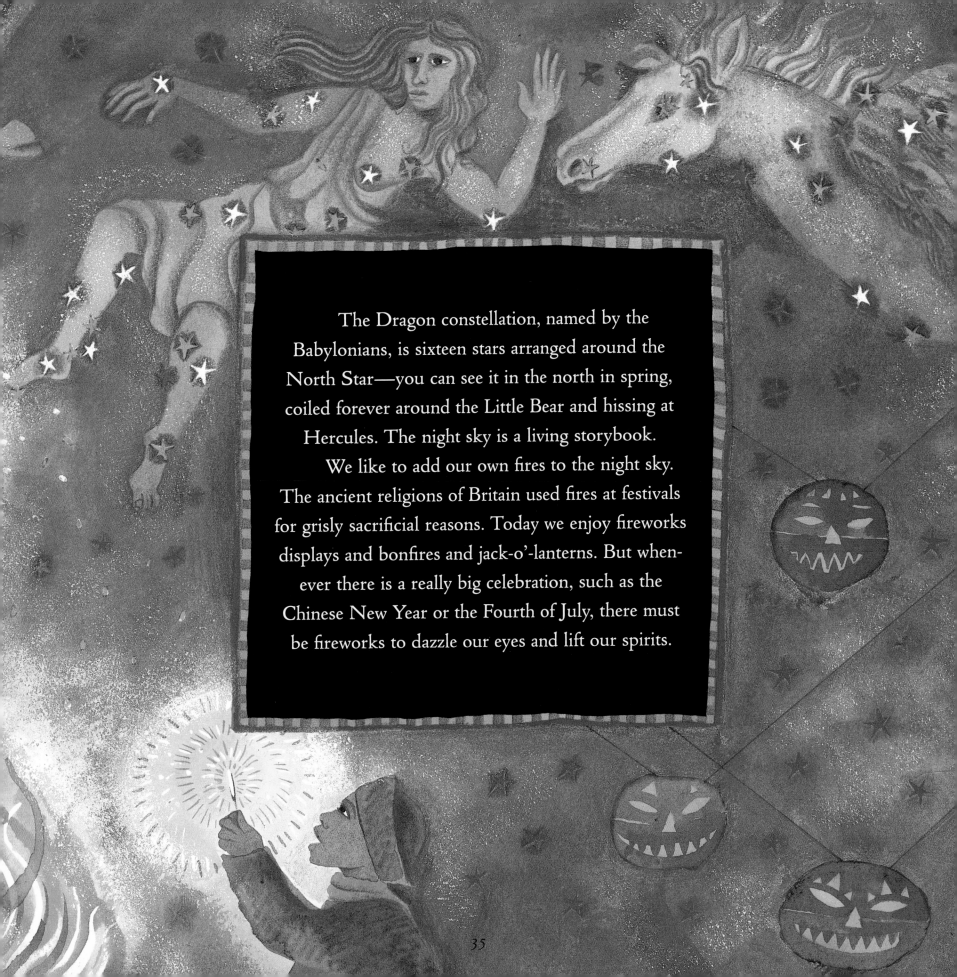

The Dragon constellation, named by the Babylonians, is sixteen stars arranged around the North Star—you can see it in the north in spring, coiled forever around the Little Bear and hissing at Hercules. The night sky is a living storybook.

We like to add our own fires to the night sky. The ancient religions of Britain used fires at festivals for grisly sacrificial reasons. Today we enjoy fireworks displays and bonfires and jack-o'-lanterns. But whenever there is a really big celebration, such as the Chinese New Year or the Fourth of July, there must be fireworks to dazzle our eyes and lift our spirits.

FIRE WORSHIP

The first people to make fire lived in China about 400,000 years ago. That may seem a long time, but it is recent compared with how long the other three elements have influenced human life. Earth, water, and air are all around us, but fire occurs on its own in nature only occasionally. Perhaps this accounts for the importance of fire in ancient mythologies.

In many parts of the world the first gods to be worshiped were sun gods, powerful fire beings who were thought to live inside the sun. The supreme god of the Egyptians was Ra, who shared his qualities with whoever was king at the time. In India, Surya, "the eye of heaven," and Savitri were both sun gods. Parsis of Iran and India still worship Ahura Mazda and have sacred ceremonies involving flames.

Sun gods are usually male. Because
the sun disappears below the horizon at
each dusk and rises with the dawn each morning,
many people believed in a fiery god who died every night and
came back to life every morning. Ra, for example, steered across
the heavens in a boat, pursued by a huge crocodile, which
seemed to devour the sun at the end of the day. The reappear-
ance of the sun in the morning was a sign that Ra had killed
the crocodile once more.

STEALING FIRE

There are many stories about how people learned to make fire from the gods or whoever else was its keeper. The Native Americans in what is now Canada told a story that it was Bear who had the secret of fire. He kept a firestone tied to his belt and used it to make sparks.

One day when Bear was relaxing in his cave in front of a fire, a cold little bird hopped in and asked to be warmed. The gruff bear consented—in return for the bird's picking lice out of his fur. This she did, but every now and again she also pecked at the thong holding the firestone. As soon as the thong was pecked through, she snatched the stone and flew away. Outside the cave, a long line of animals passed the magic stone as quickly as possible from one to the other. The last was Fox. He ran to the top of a mountain and dashed the stone to pieces. He threw a fragment to each of the tribes. And that is how native North Americans learned to make fire.

FIREBIRDS AND DRAGONS

Fire has its own mythical creatures. The legendary salamander was able to live unharmed inside a fire. The Egyptian phoenix was an extraordinary bird that represented the sun—there was only one phoenix at any time. With red and gold feathers, it was a beautiful bird believed to live for a thousand years. When the time came for it to die, it built its own funeral pyre out of spiced wood, and the sun's rays set fire to it. A new phoenix was born from the ashes of the fire, symbolizing new life and hope.

The fire creature we know best is the dragon. There are as many stories about it as about the unicorn. Perhaps they grew out of people's glimpses of giant lizards. From stories and pictures, we know what a traditional European dragon looks like without ever having seen one—a huge scaly serpent with wings and a long reptilian tail. It has fearsome teeth, a forked tongue, and huge nostrils, out of which it breathes flame. The dragon's traditional food is young maidens, and its enemy a hero with a sword. The only dragon that doesn't fit this description is the Chinese dragon, which is a water creature.

THE ETERNAL FLAME

Ηow many miles to Babylon?
Threescore miles and ten.
Can I get there by candlelight?
Yes and back again.

Candlelight takes you to places you normally only dream of. It has a magical quality, fending off the dark while you hold it in your hand like a talisman. There is traditionally something sacred about a single flame; Christian churches use candles in processions and on the altar. But the tradition is still older: In ancient Rome there was a temple to the goddess Vesta, who was in charge of the sacred flame of the hearth. Vesta had taken a vow to remain unmarried all her life. The young women who came and served in her

temple followed her example and were known as vestal virgins. A single flame is often a symbol of a single soul. Catholics light candles for the souls of the dead, and eternal flames are kept burning on many tombs of the unknown soldier, memorials to those who have fought and died in wars. When the Olympic Games begin, the high point of the opening ceremony is the carrying in of the torch to ignite the Olympic flame; this flame will be kept burning throughout the games.

At Eastertime in many Mediterranean countries, there are processions up to high places of worship. The processions are held in the warm, flower-scented dark, with every person in the village or town climbing a hill and carrying a torch or candle. At midnight on Easter Saturday, the vigil comes to an end with the lighting of the huge paschal candle, from which lots of new small ones are lit to

FUNERAL FIRES

Celebrating a birth or mourning a death are times when people feel closest to the elements. Like earth, fire has a part to play in the rituals surrounding death. Hindus build funeral pyres and have strong beliefs about which member of the dead person's family should light the fires. Viking heroes were launched out to sea on their ships; the ships were set on fire as they slipped into the water. Only a very great warrior or chieftain received this treatment, since the ships were of great value. The dead man's richest belongings were also destroyed with him.

At a burial of the Norse god Balder, his horse was
slaughtered and thrown into the ship; his wife,
who had died of a broken heart,
was burned with him.

Though it may seem a long way from a Viking hero's funeral, many people today also
have their bodies burned, or cremated, when they die. The fire is thought to symbolize the
purification of the body. Some people even ask for their ashes to be scattered in a place they
loved during their lifetime.

A Bad Master

Fire is said to be "a good servant but a bad master." In other words, we enjoy all the warmth and comfort and cooked food that fire provides. But we are terrified of fire when it gets out of hand. Perhaps this is because we have never really had mastery of it. Even the planned burning of woodlands and forests brings results beyond human control. Once the trees have gone, the fertile topsoil can disappear, and gradually the land can become a desert where nothing grows.

But the old idea of fire living in the sun gives us new hope for the planet, too. We can use the energy that comes from the sun—solar energy—instead of burning wood and fossil fuels for power. Solar energy can warm our homes and heat our water and perhaps cook our food and propel our cars. So we are developing a new way to come close to one of the traditional spirits of fire.

THE SEA

Human beings are made up of nearly three-quarters water. Earth, our planet, has twice as much water as land. Perhaps this is why we are so fascinated by the sea. Its salt water is undrinkable to us, but it yields a fine harvest of food to anyone brave enough to risk its unpredictable moods. Whether calmly sparkling in the sun or towering in terrifying waves, the sea draws us to it. It has given birth to more stories, poems, superstitions, and works of art and music than perhaps any other element. From ancient times, the desire to explore its vast deeps and expanses has led to perilous adventures. Herodotus wrote, 2,500 years ago, "There are the living, the dead, and those who voyage on the sea."

47

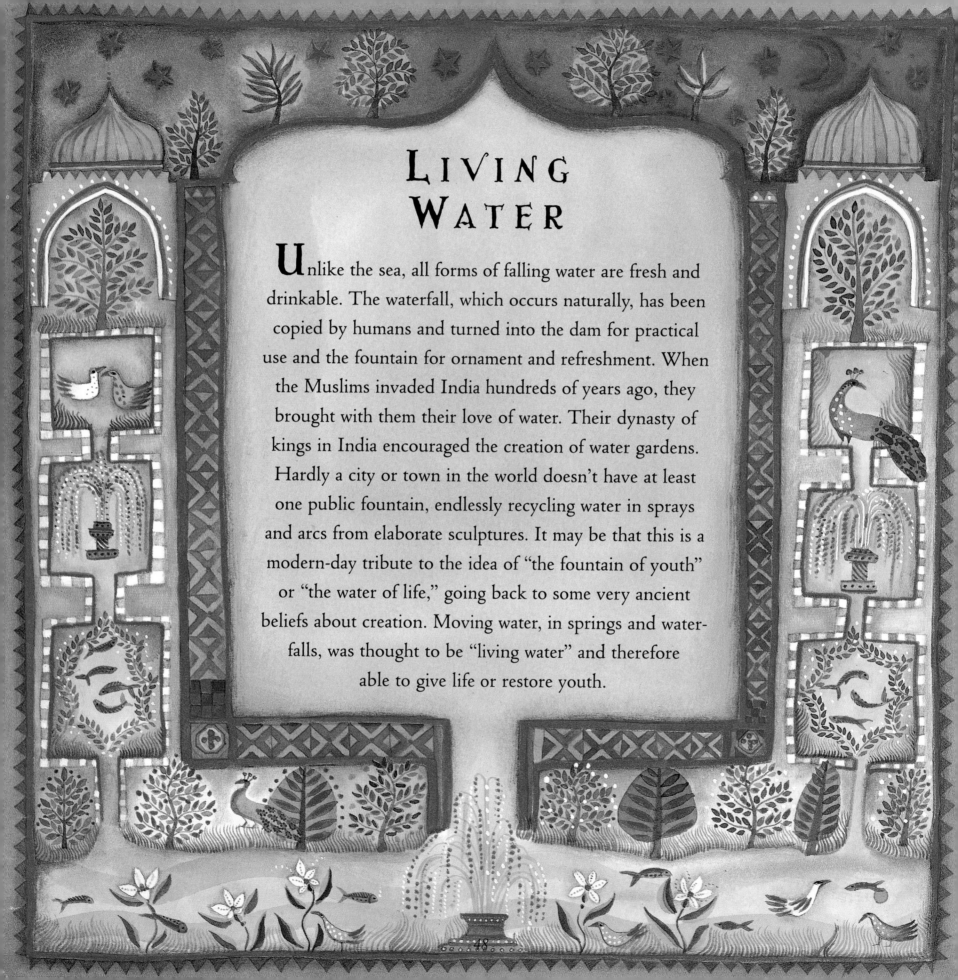

LIVING WATER

Unlike the sea, all forms of falling water are fresh and drinkable. The waterfall, which occurs naturally, has been copied by humans and turned into the dam for practical use and the fountain for ornament and refreshment. When the Muslims invaded India hundreds of years ago, they brought with them their love of water. Their dynasty of kings in India encouraged the creation of water gardens. Hardly a city or town in the world doesn't have at least one public fountain, endlessly recycling water in sprays and arcs from elaborate sculptures. It may be that this is a modern-day tribute to the idea of "the fountain of youth" or "the water of life," going back to some very ancient beliefs about creation. Moving water, in springs and waterfalls, was thought to be "living water" and therefore able to give life or restore youth.

Like earth, water is a female element, closely associated with fertility and childbirth. In Mexico, the washing of newborn babies was once accompanied by chants to the water goddess, who was celebrated as the child's real mother. Early ancestors of the Finns and Hungarians prayed to a water mother when they wanted children. And in The Gambia today, women with fertility problems may visit sacred crocodile pools and bathe themselves with the water before praying to be given children.

49

FISHES

There is something very mysterious about creatures that can live in the element of water. Some, like fishes, can breathe underwater and spend their whole lives there. To them our element of air means death. Others, sea mammals such as whales and walruses, have to come up for air eventually. But apart from that, these relatives of ours are perfectly adapted to their element, having sleek bodies and powerful muscles that allow them to swim as well as fish. Sharks never sleep; their whole lives are spent on the move in the water.

The tiny fish enjoy themselves
in the sea.
Quick little splinters of life,
their little lives are fun to them
in the sea.

D. H. LAWRENCE

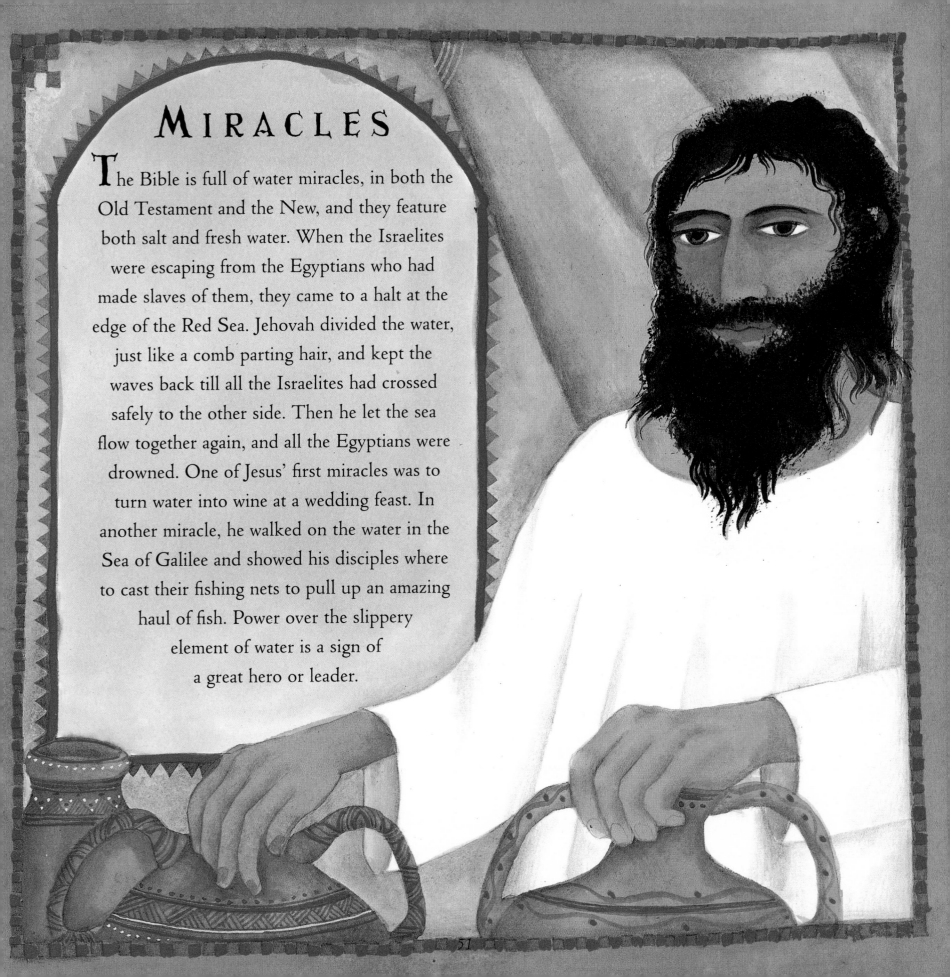

MIRACLES

The Bible is full of water miracles, in both the Old Testament and the New, and they feature both salt and fresh water. When the Israelites were escaping from the Egyptians who had made slaves of them, they came to a halt at the edge of the Red Sea. Jehovah divided the water, just like a comb parting hair, and kept the waves back till all the Israelites had crossed safely to the other side. Then he let the sea flow together again, and all the Egyptians were drowned. One of Jesus' first miracles was to turn water into wine at a wedding feast. In another miracle, he walked on the water in the Sea of Galilee and showed his disciples where to cast their fishing nets to pull up an amazing haul of fish. Power over the slippery element of water is a sign of a great hero or leader.

HOLY WATER

The unicorn is also said to have had power over water. It could cleanse the most poisonous and polluted water by dipping its long horn in it. Native North Americans, along with many other peoples, tried to gain power over water by chanting and performing ritual dances to make the rain come. A Navajo rain chant begins:

Far as man can see,
Comes the rain,
Comes the rain with me.

From the Rain-Mount,
Rain-Mount far away,
Comes the rain,
Comes the rain with me.

When the rain did come, the people gave thanks.

Many religions still use water as part of their ceremonies. In the Christian church, new members are baptized with holy water; they may even be completely submerged in a small pool. Dipping in water symbolizes the old life being washed away and a new life beginning.

In India, the Hindus regard the whole long river Ganges as sacred. Washing in its waters is supposed to bring good fortune, especially in the holy city of Benares. But even though the river is holy, people still wash their clothes and themselves in it. Refuse is emptied into the river and bodies are floated down it. The spirit of the Ganges is thought to be great enough to withstand any pollution.

MERMAIDS

There are many stories of creatures living in the water who are stranger than any real ones. The most persistent legend is the mermaid. According to tradition, she is a beautiful young woman with golden hair and a comb and mirror, but from the waist down she is all fish. She is the undoing of many sailors, enticing them into deep water with her singing. The whole idea of mermaids probably originated from sailors' tales of the dugong, a sea mammal that suckles its young in an upright position in the water. So the image of the lovely, seductive mermaid may come from a rather homely sea cow.

Greek legends are full of stories of tritons and sea nymphs ruled over by the great god of the sea, Poseidon, with his long beard and trident. The stories tell of sea monsters, too, like the one who was going to eat the princess Andromeda till Perseus rescued her. The belief in water monsters is still common. Many people think there is a monster in Loch Ness.

THE FLOOD

Water is so unpredictable and so frightening when it has been whipped up by storms that it is easy to see where the idea of sea monsters comes from. Storms and torrential rains are as destructive as fire and can move as fast. Tidal waves, caused by undersea earthquakes and volcanoes, travel with horrific speed and crash onto the land, killing people and animals and ruining whole cities.

Many countries all over the world have stories of a Great Flood that wiped out all the people on earth except one family.

From that family the earth was given a fresh start, and a whole new race of people was born. The story is so widespread that some historians think there once was such a universal flooding. The earliest version is found in an inscription from about 4,000 years ago in Mesopotamia, in which the survivor was not an ordinary good man like Noah but a great king called Ziusudra. He dreamed that the gods were cursing the earth, and so he built a boat.

All the windstorms of immense power, they all came together.
The rainstorm raged along with them.
And when for seven days and seven nights
The rainstorm in the land had raged,
The huge boat on the great waters by the windstorm had been carried away.
Utu, the sun, came forth, shedding light over heaven and earth. . . .

DROWNED ATLANTIS

Whether or not there was a flood over the whole world, there were certainly many disturbances in the waters of the Mediterranean in ancient times. Earthquakes and volcanoes led to tidal waves, one of which is famous for overwhelming the city of Atlantis.

For a long time the story of lost Atlantis, a great city under the water, seemed to be just a myth, based on an Egyptian story that was later written down by the Greek philosopher Plato. His portrait of the island kingdom of Atlantis was very detailed, describing the main city of this great civilization as built on a hilltop surrounded by three circles of seawater and two of land. According to Plato, the island had been given to the god Poseidon, whose sons ruled there for generations. It was a great power, rich in crops and trade and possessing a strong army.

Then suddenly, in the course of a day and a night, the whole island was destroyed and its civilization wiped out as if it had never been.

Now archaeologists have found remains on the Aegean island of Santorini that show that a great and prosperous Minoan city once flourished there. It was destroyed in 1500 B.C. by an earthquake, which sent tidal waves as far as northern Crete. There were even concentric rings found under the sea near the island. So perhaps Atlantis was a real place after all.

FREEING THE WATERS

There is no water that cannot be polluted by modern life. We have contaminated our rivers, lakes, ponds, and seas. In some places, even the rain that falls from the sky has so many chemicals in it that trees are dying.

Sometimes something that seemed like a good idea and a benefit to people, such as fertilizers to enrich poor soil, has led to pollution, as chemicals have washed off the land and into our rivers. Oil spills in the sea have killed wildlife and left a sticky black mess on our beaches. But slowly people are remembering how precious clean water is and are making laws to prevent various kinds of water pollution.

Some businesses have even started collecting rainwater in huge barrels, just as people used to a hundred years ago, to reduce the amount of water they use from reservoirs.

TAMING THE SKY

The Greeks must have spent a lot of time looking up at the sky. They told many stories of heroes who tried to conquer the air. One of them was a young man called Bellerophon. The goddess Athena helped him catch a wonderful flying horse named Pegasus.

Bellerophon did great deeds with the help of the winged horse, but in the end he grew too ambitious and tried to fly up to the gods' home on Mount Olympus.

Zeus decided to teach him a lesson. He sent a gadfly to sting Pegasus, so that the horse shied and threw Bellerophon to earth. Pegasus reached Olympus and lived there ever after.

Icarus was another young man who tried to fly. With his father,
Daedalus, he was imprisoned on the island of Crete.
Daedalus made them both wings of feathers and
wax so that they could escape by air. Daedalus
warned his son not to fly too close to the
sun, but once Icarus felt the air under
his wings, he forgot. The hot sun
melted the wax, his wings fell apart,
and Icarus plunged to his death
in the sea.

Iris was the
messenger of the
gods. A rainbow was her
stairway in the air from
Olympus to earth.

THE HOME OF THE GODS

The rainbow played a part in Norse
mythology, too. The Nordic peoples believed there was a
rainbow bridge between middle earth, where people lived, and
Asgard, the home of the gods. Across it might come Thor, the
mighty thunder god, who made storms by whirling his hammer; or
perhaps Odin, the chief god, known as the Allfather.

Odin was a great sky god. He rode an eight-legged horse called Sleipnir and had two pet ravens whose names meant Thought and Memory. They flew through the air carrying messages to and from the Allfather.

Odin built a great palace in Asgard called Valhalla. The Valkyries did his bidding there. They were powerful warrior-women who flew through the skies above battlefields, collecting dead heroes whom they brought back to Valhalla to make a strong army to defend Odin against his enemies.

THUNDERBIRDS AND STARPEOPLE

In North America, the people of the lakes and plains looked up at the magnificent golden eagles and other birds that whirled through the air and thought they must be winged spirits. The Algonquins believed that the beating of birds' wings caused the winds. The tribes of the Northwest believed in winged gods called Thunderbirds. They thought that lightning was the flash of a Thunderbird's eye.

Many native North Americans believed in a Star Country where beautiful beings lived high above the earth. Sometimes a Starmaiden would spy a handsome brave and come down to earth in disguise. She would take him back up to her own country. Or sometimes it was the beauty of a mortal woman that caught the eye of one of the Star-youths. But the story always ended the same way.

The Starpeople could marry mortals and have children with them. All was well as long as the humans were content to live up in the Star Country with their loved ones. But eventually the humans would get homesick and want to revisit their own people. Even then, all could be well as long as they told no one about their life with the Starpeople. Alas, the humans were always tempted into telling, and then they could never go back.

WINGED CREATURES

Everyone can imagine how wonderful it must be to have wings and be able to fly. But for the creatures that do, life is hard; they spend most of their time searching for food. A little bird must eat several times its own body weight every day to stay alive. Big birds like hawks and owls have to catch fast-moving little creatures to eat.

There
are thousands of different
kinds of birds, from the hedge sparrow to the
giant condor, and there are millions of different kinds of insects. Many of them can fly,
too. Butterflies, dragonflies, damselflies, and
ladybugs all live a very short life compared
with people, and they spend most of it on the
wing. Within days, sometimes within hours,
many of them must eat, mate, and leave eggs
to grow into more winged creatures like
themselves.

ANGELS AND DEVILS

Perhaps it is because people can fly only in their minds that we have invented so many creatures with wings. The angels and archangels of Christianity can be powerful and frightening, like stern Michael with his flaming sword, standing guard at the gate of Eden to stop Adam and Eve from getting back in. Less frightening are the chubby little cherubs that painters of five hundred years ago put into their pictures of Jesus and his mother. Smaller than cherubs are the tiny creatures with butterfly wings who are the fairies of fairy stories.

The devil was an angel once, too—Lucifer, the light bringer. There are many imaginary winged creatures that are wicked: vampires, like Count Dracula, and demons, like Ravana, who stole Sita from Rama in the Hindu story of the Ramayana. Ravana had ten heads and twenty arms, but Rama managed to track him down and kill him with the help of another air spirit, the great bird Jatayu.

RED SKY AT NIGHT

The one aspect of the elements that every person is still in touch with is the weather. For some, the weather is a vital question. Will there be rain to make crops grow, or will there be fair weather for safe fishing? For others, it is just a matter of carrying an umbrella or hoping for sunshine on the beach. But we all look up at the sky and sense from the air what the weather will be.

Meteorologists use very sophisticated instruments and calculations for predicting the weather. But since they often get it wrong, we may prefer traditional customs of forecasting the weather from colors in the sky or the behavior of animals.

There are many folk sayings about the weather, a number of them based on the look of the sky. Some actually agree with scientific explanations about cloud formations. The sayings were all based on observations, handed down over generations, long before there was any science of meteorology.

A rainbow in the morning is a sailor's warning.
　A rainbow at night is a sailor's delight.

~

Evening red and morning gray,
　Help the traveler on his way.
Evening gray and morning red,
　Bring down rain upon his head.

~

Red sky at night, shepherd's delight.
　Red sky in the morning, shepherd's warning.

~

When clouds appear like rocks and towers,
　The earth's refreshed by frequent showers.

~

If woolly fleeces spread the heavenly way,
　No rain, be sure, disturbs the summer's day.

~

Mackerel scales and mare's tails
　Make lofty ships carry low sails.

~

When the wind is in the north,
　The skillful fisher goes not forth.
When the wind is in the east,
　It is good for neither man nor beast.
When the wind is in the south,
　It blows your bait into a fish's mouth.
When the wind is in the west,
　Then the weather is at its best.

~

HURRICANES AND TORNADOES

The air around us can become as terrifying as any other of the four elements if we live in countries where there are hurricanes and typhoons. These are violent tropical storms with winds that travel up to 220 miles per hour (360 kph). What begins as a small thunderstorm over the warm ocean builds up into a spinning circle sucking up warm air. By the time it reaches land, it is an outer circle of devastating winds with a calm "eye" at the center. Tornadoes, or twisters, move even faster than hurricanes.

They can cause terrible destruction in minutes, hurling trees, roofs, and even people up into the air and carrying them long distances before flinging them down again. The tornado starts in a storm, when warm air is sucked up into a column of swirling wind. A long funnel of twisting air hangs down from the thundercloud, and when it touches the earth, the powerful vacuum sucks up everything in its path.

A Breath of Fresh Air

Air is the most easily polluted element of all. The air in a small, closed room can quickly fill up with cigarette smoke or aerosol fumes. Out in the open, in the vastness of the sky, we find it hard to believe that the air cannot somehow cleanse itself. But it cannot, and one result is now a hole that appears over the Antarctic every spring in the earth's ozone layer. The ozone layer protects us from the harmful rays of the sun that cause skin cancer, so it is very important to stop that hole from getting any bigger.

Just as we respect the other elements, we have to respect the air around us. We need to try to drive our cars less, try not to use aerosols with CFCs, to recycle as much trash as possible instead of burning it, to make smoking tobacco a thing of the past, and to campaign to stop the rain forests from being cut down, for they are an important source of the oxygen we all breathe.

Every little bit helps. People can regain a closer and more harmonious relationship with the elements. We can remember how vital earth, fire, water, and air are to human life. We can acknowledge what powerful influences they have been on people in the past and what great art they have inspired. And with every small step to help one of the four elements, a little of the magic they have lost is returned to them. One day, if we learn to treat them as friends, not enemies, earth, fire, water, and air may regain the beauty and power they had when the world began.

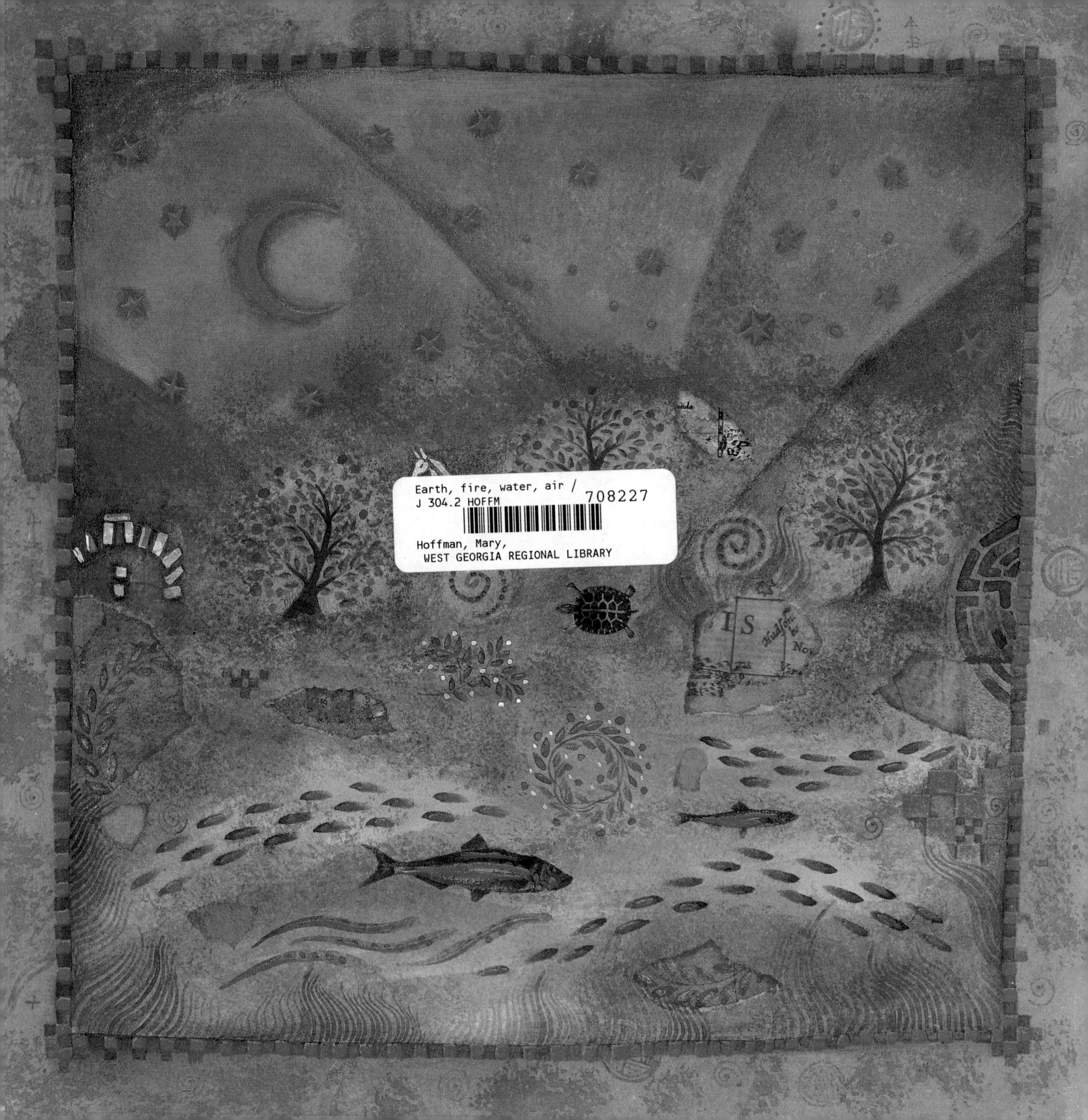